Happy Birthday
Linda Lou,
Love
Dianne, Frank
Justin

Best Wishes
Brian B.

Discovering Newfoundland

Brian C. Bursey

ISBN 0-921191-78-2

Cover photo: Petites, an isolated fishing community on the Southwest Coast.

Canadian Cataloguing in Publication Data

Bursey, Brian C.
   Discovering Newfoundland
   ISBN 0-921191-78-2
1. Newfoundland -- Pictorial works. I. Title
FC2162.B87 1993   971.8'04'0222   C93-098555-9
F1122.8.B87 1993

Second Printing 1997

Printed in Canada

INTRODUCTION

Photographers have taken many beautiful pictures in Newfoundland, some of which have been published in books which are to be treasured. To anyone who travels the remote areas of this island, however, it is obvious that a great many more books will not exhaust the interesting material still to be photographed.

The pictures in this book are the result of many years of wilderness travel; hunting with a camera through the forests and barrens of Newfoundland's interior by canoe or on foot, or along the coast. It is the book of a wanderer who is aware that the best of Newfoundland is still comparatively unknown.

Captured here are aspects of Newfoundland which are less accessible and more subtle in flavour than those seen by the tourist or the Newfoundlander who remains close to the larger centers. To a great extent, the appeal of Newfoundland is its unspoiled environment, many aspects of which are captured in these photographs, from the tiny woodland mushroom, *russula integra*, to the magnificent humpback whale.

Here too, are pictures of industries of the past, now part of a largely forgotten history, being slowly reclaimed by nature. Pictures of beautiful forsaken places, such as Exploits, which were thriving, vibrant Newfoundland communities where a unique life-style flourished, are reminders of a Newfoundland which is rapidly disappearing.

It is the author's hope that this book will add to the reader's understanding and appreciation of what makes Newfoundland one of the special places of the world.

For Laurel, Forrest, and Erin

Discovering Newfoundland

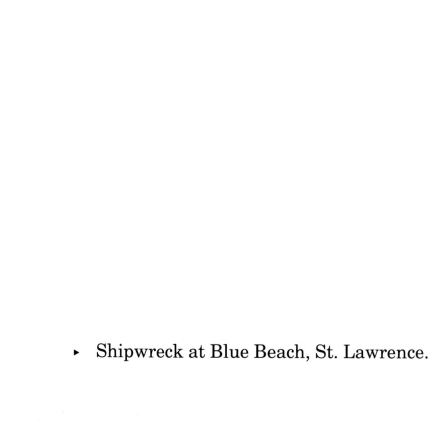

▸ Shipwreck at Blue Beach, St. Lawrence.

Abandoned iron mines, Bell Island. The presence of iron-bearing rocks at Bell Island was first noted by John Guy in the early 1600s. It was not until 1895, however, that mining began. Once the surface layer had been exhausted, work began on a second ore body, located at tidewater on the west side of the island, using room and pillar technology (above). The workings were eventually extended more than three miles under Conception Bay and, for a time, these mines were the largest iron ore producers in the British Empire. Increasing costs and changing technology, rather than exhaustion of the ore supply, led to closure in 1966.

▸ Lighthouse at Redmonds Head, Bell Island.

Tombstone, Placentia. Although frequented by Basque fishermen from the early 1500s, France did not formally establish a colony at Placentia until 1662. Easy to defend, and blessed with an excellent harbour, it was not only the centre of the French fishery in Newfoundland, but also a base for attacks on English settlements. Never captured, Placentia and other French holdings in Newfoundland were ceded to Britain by the Treaty of Utrecht of 1713.

Barracks at Queen's Battery, Signal Hill. This two-room barracks, with a capacity to house up to 19 soldiers, was constructed in the early 1830s.

Point La Haye, St. Mary's Bay. Large salt water ponds, such as this one to the right of the beach, are commonly known as 'barachois', 'barasways', or 'barachoix' in southern and western Newfoundland.

◄ Lighthouse at North Head, Bay Bulls.

Hermit crab. These small soft-shelled crabs are common residents of abandoned moon shells (below) and whelks. Crabs wear these adopted homes for protection as they scavenge over the sea bottom.

Wild rose bushes, near Petty Harbour. The leaves of this common shrub turn a brilliant crimson or scarlet after a heavy frost.

October fog at Shoal Bay, south of Petty Harbour.

◄ Low sweet blueberry. This is the most common of several species of blueberry, bilberry, and huckleberry found in Newfoundland. The fruit ripen in August and remain until frost.

Lighthouse, Ferryland.

The Downs, Ferryland. Ferryland is one of Newfoundland's oldest communities, having been a centre of the English fisheries from the late 1500s. Formal attempts to establish plantations by George Calvert (later Lord Baltimore) and Sir David Kirke began in the early 1600s. Ferryland was destroyed by the Dutch in 1673 and later became a centre of conflict during the War of 1812. Abandoned cannon may still be found on the Downs and on nearby Bois Island.

Abandoned boat and boathouse on Big Pond, north of Colinet. This clinker-built boat, many miles from the nearest road, was once used in the harvesting of logs for a local sawmill.

◄ The mast of this abandoned whaling vessel in Harbour Buffett, Placentia Bay, still displays the 'barrel' from which crew members searched for far-off whales. Humpbacks, minkes, and other species are common in this area.

Air bubbles give an unusual pattern to the frozen surface of this stream.

Trouty, a small fishing community in Trinity Bay.

Cape Spear, the most easterly point in North America. Waves in excess of 30 metres may occur in Newfoundland waters after several days of strong winds.

Erratic, Avalon Peninsula. Large boulders, such as this one perched atop a small hill near Butlers Pond, are common throughout Newfoundland. Such boulders were carried across the land, often for many miles, to be eventually deposited 'erratically' by glaciers as they melted.

Red admiral butterfly. This common Newfoundland butterfly feeds on nettles.

◄ Falls on Southwest River, near Port Blandford.

◄ Burnt woods, Northwest Gander River.

Black-legged kittiwakes. Locally known as 'tickleaces', they are common on breeding cliffs during the summer months.

Norman's Cove, Trinity Bay. Chapel Head, in the background, is composed of red and grey sedimentary rock.

Partridgeberries—near Hants Harbour, Trinity Bay.

Gannets. Bird Rock at Cape St. Mary's is New-foundland's largest gannet colony. Mature gannets, 75 to 80 centimetres long and with a wingspan of 180 centimetres, are Newfound-land's largest sea birds.

Entrance to Brigus Harbour, Conception Bay.

Fresh shoots of wild grass denote the arrival of spring to the high windswept barrens of the Avalon Wilderness Area.

Gosling. Canada geese are common to remote rivers, lakes and marshes. The young are usually hatched in May. Goslings quickly lose their yellow colouring as feathers begin to emerge from their covering of down.

The Spout. This prominent landmark, located midway between Bay Bulls and Petty Harbour, occurs when waves in a nearby sea cave force saltwater and mist from a fissure in the bedrock. During heavy swells, the 'Spout' can be seen for many miles out to sea.

Pouch Cove. An offshore oil drilling rig, just visible on the horizon, provides a vivid contrast with the rustic fishing stages of the inshore fishery.

Black duck nest, Long Harbour, Fortune Bay. This down-lined nest is built underneath over-lagging branches on the shore of a small stream.

Back River, a tributary of the Colinet River.

Weather buoy, Middle Cove. These buoys are used by the offshore oil industry to collect data on wind, wave height, and ocean currents. Since oceanographic information for Newfoundland's continental shelf is limited, weather buoys are often anchored at prospective sites to monitor local conditions prior to the commencement of drilling.

◄ François at dawn. This isolated south coast fishing community cannot be reached by road.

Southport, Trinity Bay.

Iceberg near Bell Island, Conception Bay. Most Newfoundland icebergs originate from glaciers on the west coast of Greenland. This iceberg, which towers approximately 30 metres above the water, is considered medium sized. Seven-eighths of its bulk remain underwater.

Russula integra — This is a common woodland
mushroom of August-September. While this
variety is edible, the large number of similar
mushrooms can make a positive identification
difficult.

This 'gully', located west of the Salmonier Line, is typical of thousands of small ponds scattered throughout Newfoundland.

Southport, Trinity Bay.

Growler, Crow Head, North Twillingate Island.

The community of Deer Harbour, Random Island was resettled in the mid-1960s, one of 148 communities which were abandoned between 1965 and 1975, involving in total the relocation of over 20,000 people.

Traytown, Ireland's Eye Island. Between 1954 and 1975 several hundred isolated communities were resettled by the Federal and Provincial Governments in an effort to centralize population in 'growth centres' where public services, such as transportation, schools and medical care, could be more readily provided. While some existing houses were floated to growth centres, such as Arnold's Cove or Marystown, many larger buildings could not be relocated.

Humpback whale, Portugal Cove. Named for their unusually shaped dorsal fin, humpbacks are five metres long and weigh two tons at birth. Adults may exceed twelve metres in length and weigh 30-40 tons. Although still considered to be an endangered species, humpbacks are common in Newfoundland waters during the summer months, feeding primarily on caplin. Most adults winter in the Caribbean where their young are born. Immensely powerful, humpbacks will occasionally engage in spectacular displays, sometimes jumping clear of the water and slapping the surface with their fins or tails.

Water vapour from nearby open water has formed elaborate frost crystals on this newly frozen sea ice near Traytown, Bonavista Bay.

Tiger swallowtail, Exploits River. The largest
Newfoundland butterfly. This common butterfly, which feeds on birch and other deciduous
species, is often found on the damp sand and
gravel deposits along streams or in other
moist sunny areas.

▸ Paradise River. This gorge, more than 70 metres deep, was dammed in 1988 to make way
for a hydroelectric development.

Barneys Brook.

◄ Labrador retriever, Northwest River. The Labrador Retriever, despite its name, did not originate in Labrador but rather in eastern and southern Newfoundland and was sometimes referred to as the St. John's Water Dog. Forerunners of the present breed were used to retrieve sea birds, as well as codfish which slipped from the hook on the surface of the water.

Terra Nova River, below Mollyguajeck Lake.

This particularly large glacial boulder or 'erratic' is located about 15 kilometres east of Kepenkeck Lake.

▸ The pink lady's slipper, or moccasin flower, is found in a variety of habitats throughout Newfoundland.

Wild roses, such as this specimen near Cape Broyle, are a common late summer flower.

Port Elizabeth, Placentia Bay. The communities of Port Elizabeth and nearby Flat Island were originally settled in the early 1800s. The population reached a peak of almost 500 in 1874 before entering a period of prolonged decline. The remaining families were resettled in Red Harbour and other Burin Peninsula communities between 1969 and 1971.

◄ Osprey nest, Piper's Hole River.

Pintail duck, male. Pintails are found in ponds and marshes, where they feed in shallow water.

American widgeon (baldpate), male. This species, seldom seen in Newfoundland, feeds primarily on aquatic vegetation.

Steam engine at Main Point, Gander Bay.
Sawmilling and pulpwood harvesting con-
tinue to be important industries in this area.

Cod liver oil, Job's Cove. Cod livers are rich in Vitamin A and were once highly valued as a remedy for everything from the common cold to tuberculosis. In addition, cod liver oil had extensive industrial uses as an organic lubricant and in the tannery industry. While the production of cod liver oil was once a major industry, contributing at least 10 per cent of the value of total Newfoundland exports in the mid-1800s, demand declined thereafter due to the development of vegetable oils as a cheap and effective substitute. Most cod liver oil was produced by throwing the livers into barrels or steel drums where they were allowed to decompose.

Northwest River, near Port Blandford.

Moose. This non-indigenous species was first introduced to the Island in 1878. Uncertainty about the success of this initial effort led to a second introduction in 1904. A series of forest fires during the twentieth century and large cutover areas from pulpwood harvesting have created ideal feeding areas for moose, encouraging rapid dispersal and propagation. Nevertheless, moose were not reported on the Avalon Peninsula until 1941. The current population numbers about 50,000 animals.

Clavaria. This unusual flesh-coloured specimen, popularly referred to as 'coral fungi', is a member of the *Clavariaceae* family.

Pleurotus porrigens. This delicate mushroom grows on rotting conifers.

Exploits, Notre Dame Bay. During the mid-1800s, the community of Exploits was a major fishing and commercial centre of Notre Dame Bay. A decline in traditional industries led to a substantial loss in population from the Depression onwards and most remaining residents were resettled during the 1960s and '70s.

British Harbour, Trinity Bay.

The Arch, Arch Tickle, near Salvage, Bonavista Bay.

Reflectors, Cape Bonavista Lighthouse. This lighthouse, erected in 1843, contains 200 year old lights which had been previously installed on Scotland's Inch Cape Rock. The lights, which were replaced by automatic equipment in 1962, have now been restored as part of the Cape Bonavista provincial historic site. Many early lighthouses burned seal oil as a source of light.

Sandy Cove, Eastport Peninsula. This sandy
beach is just one of several in the Eastport
area.

Bonavista. The Ryan Property, constructed in the early 1800s, is in the background. This collection of buildings, including fish processing facilities, wharves, storage sheds, and a retail outlet, is typical of the merchant operations which once dominated many Newfoundland outports.

Abandoned woods camp near Triton Brook. Privacy was at a premium for users of this four-hole privy.

◄ Tea Arm, Notre Dame Bay. This outcropping in Tea Arm, north of Point Leamington, owes its distinctive colour to the oxidation of iron pyrite contained in the rock.

Red and mountain maples are common in central and western Newfoundland, particularly along streams and on moist slopes. Neither species has any commercial importance, rarely exceeding 12 metres in height.

▸ Church, Port au Port.

Barnacles, such as these on the head of
beached humpback, are a common
parasite of large whales.

Pacquet. Unusually heavy arctic ice in July, 1991, results in a precarious mooring for this trap boat.

Apricot jelly. The *tremellales*, or jelly fungi, can be recognized by their gelatinous or jelly-like appearance. While a number of varieties are found in Newfoundland, the large and brightly coloured apricot jelly is rare. Specimens are usually found on disturbed ground in the presence of rotting wood, making pulpwood cutting areas good locations for collecting these edible fungi.

Lobster Cove Head Lighthouse, Bonne Bay.

▸ S.S. *Kyle*, Harbour Grace. Built in 1913, the *Kyle* served on the Port aux Basques-North Sydney run and later became a prominent feature of the coastal service between Newfoundland and Labrador. Prior to 1967, when it sustained extensive ice damage, the *Kyle* was one of the oldest steam powered vessels still in commercial service. The vessel has lain derelict at Riverhead, Harbour Grace, since that time.

Caribou, Great Gull River. Its feeding inter-
rupted, this stag caribou stares suspiciously.

Mushrooms, Terra Nova Park.

Tilting, Fogo Island.

▸ Fogo, as viewed from Bleak House. Two harbours, and a proximity to rich cod and seal resources, led to the development of Fogo as a major fishing and commercial centre. One of the oldest settlements of the northeast coast, Fogo had a sizeable permanent population by the early 1700s.

Roseroot (*sedum roseum*), Quirpon Island. This is a common seashore plant
of northern Newfoundland.

◄ Fishing vessels at Little Port, Bay of Islands.

The Success Grinder, Campbellton, Notre Dame Bay. In 1911 a small sulphite pulp mill, with a capacity of 4,500 tons per year, was constructed at Campbellton by the Horwood Lumber Company of St. John's. Hydroelectric power for the mill was supplied by a dam on nearby Indian Arm River until its collapse in 1915. The dam was rebuilt but burst again the following year, leading to the closure of the operations. Remains of the mill and nearby dam are still readily visible in Campbellton.

Debarking Drums. Tommy's Arm, Notre Dame Bay. Large quantities of pulpwood have been cut throughout Newfoundland and Labrador for export to the United Kingdom and Scandinavia. Most countries require the bark to be removed from any wood imported to prevent the entry of undesirable insects and disease.

Southwest River. Running water has cut a deep channel through the varicoloured shale beds of this area.

An April growth of new moss takes on the characteristics of thickly wooded hills.

Wild rose in autumn. Both the Virginia rose and the similar northeastern rose are found in Newfoundland. The two species are common to moist, unshaded locations.

Belle Bay near Rencontre East.

Pool's Cove, Fortune Bay.

Tombstone of Rev. John Clinch, who died in Trinity in 1819. Clinch, a friend of Doctor Edward Jenner, introduced smallpox vaccination to North America at Trinity in 1800. He also collected a glossary of Beothuk terms.

Railway underpass at Port Blandford, Newfoundland. Construction of a rail line across Newfoundland began at St. John's in 1881, eventually reaching Port aux Basques in 1898. The development of alternate transportation systems and massive operating losses resulted in the closure of the railroad in September, 1988.

Iceberg, Notre Dame Bay.

The Whale Cave, near Raleigh. The Whale
Cave, or Big Oven, is one of the largest sea
caves in the world. The cave is 20 metres wide
by 15 high at the entrance and extends
inward for a distance of 100 metres.

One of several varieties of *lactarius* mushrooms found on bogs and in coniferous woods.

Clusters of various varieties of *pleurotus* fungi
grow on dead and decaying trees and stumps,
particularly in August and September.

Shoreline at Piccadilly, Port au Port Peninsula.

Port au Port Peninsula. Homemade wooden winches are in common use at fishing communities along the West Coast.

◄ Gypsum cliffs along Romaines Brook, near Stephenville.

Marsh marigolds, Port au Port Peninsula.

Rock ptarmigan, Long Range Mountains. These birds, slightly smaller than willow ptarmigan, are common to high barren hilltops in western Newfoundland. Their colouring, almost snow white in winter changing to mottled brown or grey in summer, provides excellent camouflage.

Western Brook Pond. The waterfall in the background, plunging over 600-metre cliffs, is one of North America's highest.

The Tablelands, Gros Morne National Park. This area owes its distinct colouration to peridotite, a rusty brown rock which is toxic to most forms of vegetation. Peridotite, formed deep within the earth's crust, has been forced to the surface in western Newfoundland through 'plate tectonics' or the collision of the vast continental plates which make up the earth's crust. This unusual exposure was a prime reason for the designation of the Gros Morne area as a World Heritage Site by UNESCO.

◄ Moss- and lichen- covered stump, Long Range Mountains.

The author trudges across peridotite barrens on top of Table Mountain, Gros Morne National Park.

◄ Oil well, Parson's Pond. Small deposits of crude oil were briefly exploited at Parson's Pond and on the Port au Port Peninsula around 1900. The oil was used as fuel for kerosene lamps, as a cough remedy, and for a variety of other purposes.

Green Garden, Gros Morne National Park.
Exposed sea stacks and pillow lavas, formed
when molten rock meets cold sea water,
characterize this area just north of Trout
River.

Sand dunes near Western Brook Pond, Great Northern Peninsula. Prevailing westerlies have driven sand dunes well inland, burying trees.

Locomotive 593. This coal-burning loco-
motive was manufactured by the Baldwin
Locomotive Works of Philadelphia in 1920
and delivered to St. John's for the sum of
$36,870. The engine, now located in Corner
Brook, was once a key attraction of nearby
Bowater Park.

▸ Steady Brook Falls, near Corner Brook, is
almost 100 metres high.

Sunset at Alder Pond, Upper Humber River.

Little Port, Bay of Islands. These flat-bottomed fishing boats, common to the Gulf of St. Lawrence, are seldom seen elsewhere.

Fall colours in Gros Morne National Park.

▸ The imprint of its passing betrays the origin of this large ice block, located at the base of a talus slope in western Newfoundland.

Caribou, Long Range Mountains south of Western Brook Pond. Mature doe caribou (left of picture) are the only female members of the deer family with antlers.

▸ Falls on Bakers Brook, Gros Morne National Park.

Long Point, Port au Port Peninsula. The Lewis Hills, the highest on the Island of Newfoundland, rise in the distance to a height of 815 metres.

The Arches Public Beach, south of Daniel's Harbour. Sightseers walking nearby provide scale to these large, sea-carved arches.

Red elderberry, near Crabbes River. The brilliant red of the fruit clusters contrasts vividly with the rich dark green leaves. This large shrub is relatively common to central and western Newfoundland.

Coprinus comatus mushrooms, western New-foundland. These mushrooms, often known as shaggy mane or inky caps, dissolve into a dark slime as they age. Younger specimens are some-times eaten.

Rope Cove Canyon, Lewis Hills. U-shaped glacial valleys are common throughout Newfoundland.

Wreck of the S.S. *Ethie*. The passenger and freight steamer *Ethie* was wrecked at Martin's Point, south of Cow Head, on December 10, 1919. A pulley system between the ship and dry land allowed all the crew and passengers to be saved, including a baby who was brought ashore in a mail bag.

Rose Blanche. The name Rose Blanche is thought to be a corruption of the French 'roche blanche' or white rock. There are numerous outcroppings of white granite in the area. Stone from nearby Petites was quarried around the turn of the century for use in the construction of the Courthouse at St. John's and in other buildings throughout Newfoundland.

Fox Roost. This small community of just over one hundred people is located a few kilometres east of Port aux Basques.

 Western Brook Pond in late winter.